READING
Triumphs

Mc
Graw
Hill **Macmillan
McGraw-Hill**

RFB&D
learning through listening

Students with print disabilities may be eligible to obtain an accessible, audio version of the pupil edition of this textbook. Please call Recording for the Blind & Dyslexic at I-800-22I-4792 for complete information.

B

The *McGraw·Hill* Companies

 Macmillan
McGraw-Hill

Published by Macmillan/McGraw-Hill, of McGraw-Hill Education, a division of
The McGraw-Hill Companies, Inc., Two Penn Plaza, New York, New York I0I2I.

Printed in the United States of America

ISBN 0-02-I920I7-6

5 6 7 8 9 07I 09 08

C O N T E N T S

5

Working with Words

Phonics

Read the words.

bag	big	can
cat	cap	fit
has	hat	pick
pig	tap	will

Words to Know

Read the words.

who	she
look	the

Read the story.

The Bag

Who has the bag?

Kim has it.

She can look in the bag.

She can tip the bag.

A bat is in the bag!

The Hat

by Elvin Low
illustrated by Diane Palmisciano

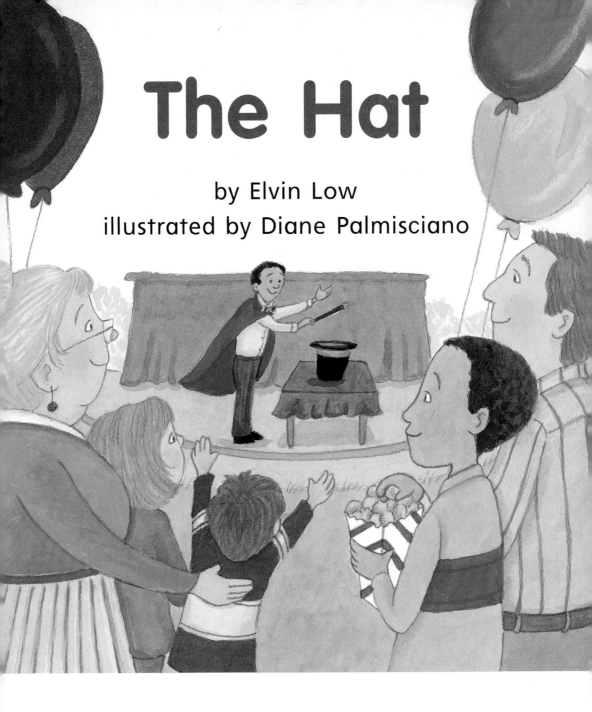

Big Jim has a hat.

Big Jim will pick Jill.
She will look in the hat.

Tap! Tap! Tap!
Who is in the hat?
A pig is in the hat!

Tap! Tap! Tap!
Who is in the hat?
Jill will look in.

A cat is in the hat!
It is as big as a pig!

Jill has the hat.
Tap! Tap! Tap!
A cap is in the hat!

Big Jim has the cap.
Will it fit Jill?

Is a pig in it?
Is a cat in it?

A duck is in the cap.
Quack! Quack! Quack!

Comprehension Check

Retell

Retell the story.
Use the pictures.

Think About It

1. Where does the story take place?
2. How do you think Jill felt at the end of the story?

Write About It

What tricks can you do?
Write about one.

Working with Words

Phonics

Read the words.

fox	egg	fed
dog	fun	mess
pup	ox	red
yes	us	yum

Words to Know

Read the words.

said	eat
you	help

Read the story.

Help Red Hen!

Bad Fox said, "Red Hen!
I will eat you up!"
Red Hen said, "Help! Help!"
Pup said, "I will help you!"
Bad Fox cannot get Red Hen.

Yum! Yum!

by Emma Rose
illustrated by Erin Mauterer

Miss Dog had eggs.

"Yum, yum, yum!" said Cat.
"Can I help?"

"Yes, yes," said Miss Dog.

"Yum, yum, yum!" said Ox.
"Can I help?"

"Yes, yes," said Miss Dog.

"Can I eat an egg?" said Fox.

"Yes, you can," said Miss Dog.

Yum, yum, yum!
The pals had fun.

It is a big mess!

"Miss Dog fed us," said Ox.

"Let us fix the mess," said Fox.

It is not a mess!
Miss Dog is happy.
The pals had fun!

Comprehension Check

Retell

Retell the story.
Use the pictures.

Think About It

1. What happened at the beginning of the story?
2. Why is Miss Dog happy at the end of the story?

Write About It

Write about a time when you shared something.

Working with Words

Phonics

Read the words.

black	flat	frog
grass	glad	swim
plop	drop	skin
slips	sniff	spot

Words to Know

Read the words.

what	this
do	some

Read the story.

A Pet Frog

What is this?

It is a pet frog.

This frog has black spots.

Do some pet frogs swim?

Yes, this frog jumped in.

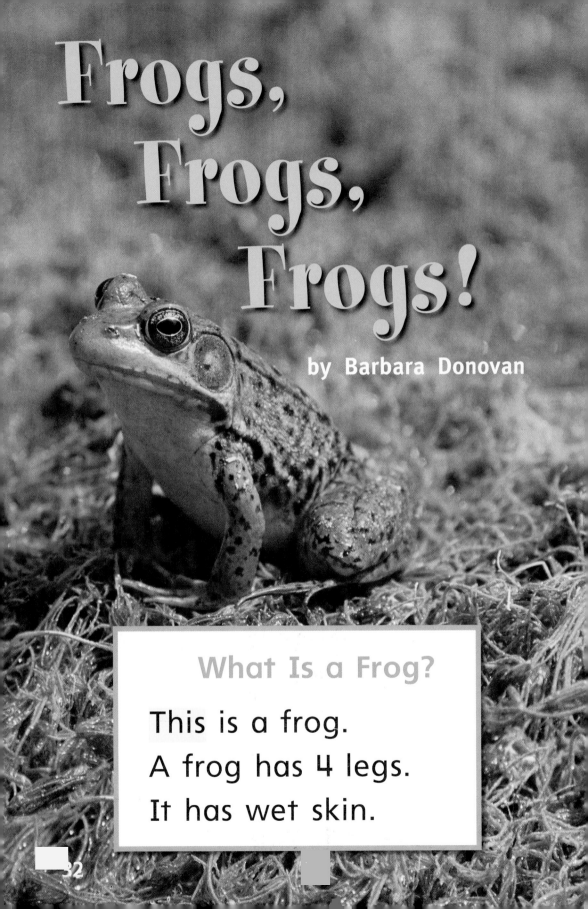

Frogs, Frogs, Frogs!

by Barbara Donovan

What Is a Frog?

This is a frog.
A frog has 4 legs.
It has wet skin.

This frog is red.
It has black spots.

What is red on this frog?

This frog is flat.
It is a water frog.

What Can Frogs Do?

Frogs can do a lot.
Frogs can hop.

Frogs can swim.
Plop! Plop!
A frog hops in the water.

Some frogs dig in mud.
Mud is wet.
The frog slips in.

A frog can sniff.
It can smell a snack.
This frog eats a bug.

Some frogs sit in grass.
Can you spot a frog?

Comprehension Check

Retell

Summarize the selection.
Use the pictures.

Think About It

1. What is this selection about?
2. Why is green a good color for frogs that live near the grass?

Write About It

Where would you go to see a real frog? Write about the place and what it is like.

Working with Words

Phonics

Read the words.

bake	cave	crane
fan	flag	game
Jane	made	spot
take	tape	wave

Words to Know

Read the words.

with	and
he	see

Read the story.

Bake a Cake!

Dave baked a cake with Dad.
Dave added nuts and eggs.
Dad baked the cake.
Then he cut it.
See the cake!

Kids Can Make It!

by Paul Ayres

illustrated by Annette Cable

Kids can make a lot!

What can kids make
with paper?

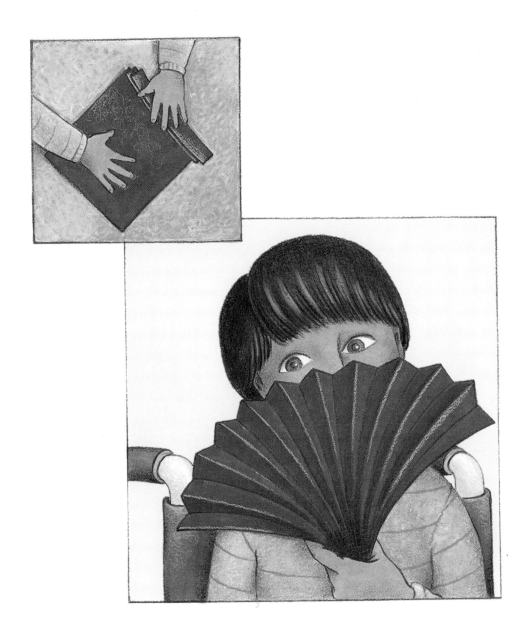

Glen had red paper.
He made a red fan.

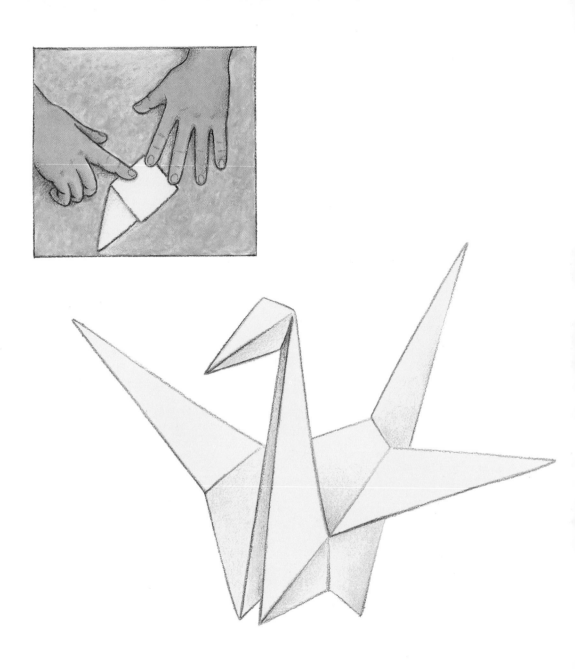

Jane did not cut.

Jane did not tape.

Jane made a crane.

Rick and Kim made a game.
Rick and Kim will get trucks.
Who will win?

What can kids make
with cloth?
Kids can make a lot!

Sal made a flag.
Sal will wave it.

Can you see Dave?
What did Dave make?
Dave made a cave!

Cam made a cape.
The kids had fun.
Kids can make a lot!

Comprehension Check

Retell

Retell the story.
Use the pictures.

Think About It

1. What is the story about?
2. How are the things the kids made different from things they could buy?

Write About It

Write about something you have made.

Working with Words

Phonics

Read the words.

bike	dive	gave
hill	is	kite
like	pig	same
in	ride	big

Words to Know

Read the words.

yellow	to
down	of

Read the story.

I Am Yellow

I am yellow.
I like to get wet.
I can dive down.
I eat a lot of bugs.
What am I?

Pig on His Bike

by Ellen Torres
illustrated by Richard Bernal

Pig sat in his pen.
He looked up.
"I see a pig on top
of the hill!" said Pig.

"It is pink like a pig," said Pig.
"It is big like a pig.
I will ride up to it."
Pig got on his red bike.

Pig met his pal, Duck.

"Look up," said Pig.

"I see a duck!" said Duck.
"It is yellow like a duck.
It dives down like a duck."

"Can I ride up to it?"
said Duck.

"Hop on!" said Pig.

Pig and Duck met Frog.

"Look up," said Pig.

"I see a frog!" said Frog.
"It hops up like a frog.
It has dots like a frog."

"Can I ride up to it?"
said Frog.

"Hop on!" said Pig.

"It is not a pig," said Pig.
"It is not a duck.
It is not a frog.
It is a big kite!"

Comprehension Check

Retell

Retell the story.
Use the pictures.

Think About It

1. What did you predict Pig
   saw? Did you change your
   mind later in the story?
2. Why did each animal see
   something different?

Write About It

What kind of kite would
you like to have?

Working with Words

Phonics

Read the words.

dome	fox	hole
home	hot	log
mine	mole	not
poke	ride	stone

Words to Know

Read the words.

where	live
under	warm

Read the story.

Ants at Home

Where do ants live?

Ants can live under logs.

Ants can live in big hills.

An ant hill is a warm home.

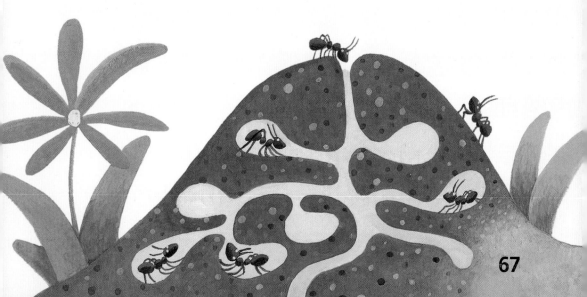

67

Animal Homes

by Rebecca Cousins

Where do animals live?
A mole has a home.
A mole lives in a hole.

A mole digs a home.
A hole is warm.
A hole is safe.

A snake has a home.
A snake can live under a stone.

The sun is hot.
A snake will not get hot
under a stone.

A fox has a home.
A fox lives in a den.
A den is a safe home.

A bat has a home.
Some bats live in caves.
Lots of bats live in this cave!

A bee is at home in a hive.
The hive looks like a dome.

Do not poke a hive.
It will make the bees mad!

Animal	Home
Mole	Hole
Ant	Hole
Fox	Den
Tiger	Den
Bat	Cave
Bear	Cave

What is an animal home?

A hole is a home.

A den is a home.

A cave is a home.

Comprehension Check

Retell

Summarize the selection.
Use the pictures.

Think About It

1. Why is a hole a good home for a mole?
2. When will the snake come out from under the stone?

Write About It

Think of an animal home.
Tell what it looks like.

Working with Words

Phonics

Read the words.

drum	fun	flute
home	hum	jug
Luke	poke	tub
tube	tune	use

Words to Know

Read the words.

have	show
play	we

Read the story.

A Fun Show

Let us have a show.
Nan can play a flute.
I can sing a tune.
We will have fun!

79

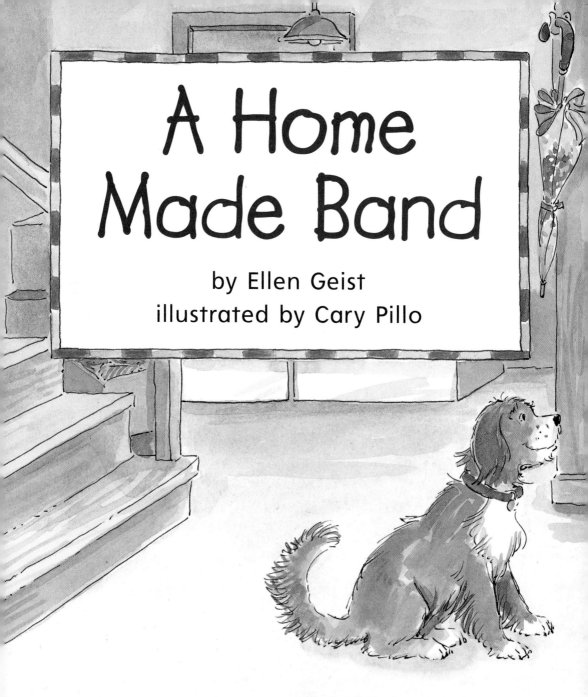

A Home Made Band

by Ellen Geist

illustrated by Cary Pillo

We will make a band.
We will have a show.

We can make up tunes.
But what can we play on?
Let us see what we can use.

Jan can use a big pot.
Jan can tap on it.
Rap-a-tap-tap!

Luke can make a flute.
He will use a tube.
He will poke holes in it.
Hum-hum-hum!

Fran has a jug.
Fran can blow into it.
Zum-zum-zum!

June will make a drum.
She can use a tub.
June will hit it.
Tick-a-tack-tack!

Sam has a bell.

He can play a tune on it.

He will make it ring.

Ting-a-ling! Ting-a-ling!

Look at Duke!
He can sing with us.
Ruff-ruff-ruff!
He can tap.
Tick-a-tack!

We will hum.
We will sing.
We will play.
This jug band is fun!
Dub-a-dub-dub!

Comprehension Check

Retell

Retell the story.
Use the pictures.

Think About It

1. What do the kids do after they have made all their instruments?
2. Why is the band special?

 Write About It

How would you make a drum? What would you use?

Working with Words

Phonics

Read the words.

best	bring	bump
cute	fast	flat
land	last	past
slope	stick	stuck

Words to Know

Read the words.

are	there
from	before

Read the story.

Pup Is Stuck

Pup is stuck.
"Are you in there?" asks Mom.
Mom lifts Pup from the box.
Next time Pup will look
before he hops in.

Who Is Best?

by Sasha Karlins
illustrated by Deborah Melmon

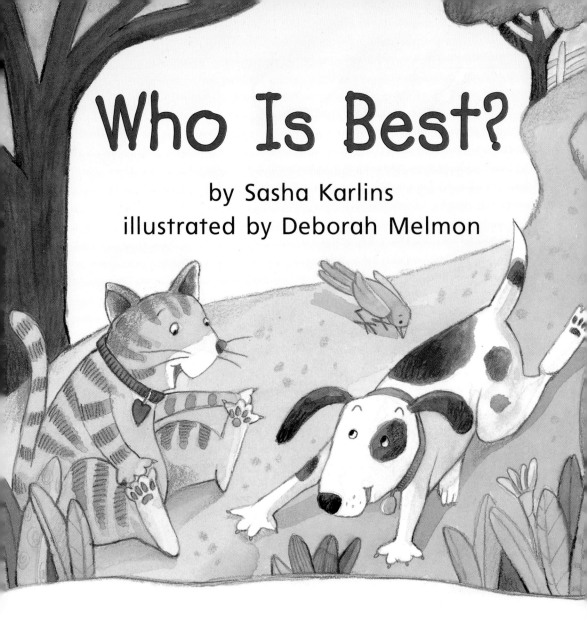

Dog and Cat liked to run.

"Let us see who is faster!"
said Dog.

Dog and Cat will run from
the pole to the gate.

"I will get there before you!"
said Cat.

Dog and Cat ran on flat land.
Dog and Cat ran up a slope.
Cat ran fast.
But Dog ran faster.

Cat hit a big stick.
Dog ran past him.
Dog hit a big bump.
Cat ran past him.

"Can you see the gate?" asked Dog. "You will get there last."

"I will not," said Cat.

Dog ran and ran.
Dog fell in a hole.

"I must help," yelled Cat.
"I will bring a stick."

Cat got a big stick.
He helped Dog grab it.

Dog and Cat ran and ran.
Cat held Dog's hand.

Dog and Cat got to the gate.
"I am best!" said Dog.

"I am best!" said Cat.

"We are best! We are friends!"
said Dog and Cat.

Comprehension Check

Retell

Retell the story.
Use the pictures.

Think About It

1. Who is faster at the beginning of the race?
2. Why does Cat help Dog instead of running past?

 Write About It

Write about a time you were in a race.

Working with Words

Phonics

Read the words.

gray	laid	left
May	plain	sand
stay	wait	went
way	rain	clay

Words to Know

Read the words.

my	four
away	good

Read the story.

A Plain Hat

"My hat is so plain," said
Gray Cat.
"I have four cute hats," said
Duck. "I can give this
hat away."
"You are a good pal!"
said Gray Cat.

The Gray Duck

by Beth Dinkin
illustrated by Jose Cruz

May Duck made a big nest.
May Duck laid four eggs.

Next, May Duck went to swim.

"Wait," May Duck quacked to the eggs.

On the way, May came to a
big egg.

"I bet this is my egg," quacked
May. "I will take it home."

Pop! Pop! Pop! Pop!
Four yellow ducks popped up.
A big gray duck popped up.

"I have five cute ducks,"
quacked May.

"Let us swim in a line,"
quacked May.

"I cannot swim in a line,"
sobbed Gray Duck.

"It is fine, my duck,"
quacked May.

"Quack, quack!" went the ducks.

"Honk, honk!" went Gray Duck.

"I cannot quack!" he sobbed.

"It is fine, my duck," quacked May.

The yellow ducks slept.
But Gray Duck did not.
Gray Duck felt sad.
He went away.

Gray Duck went to the pond.

"Look! Gray ducks just like I am!" he yelled.

"Honk! You are not a duck!" said the biggest. "You are a gray goose, just like us!"

Gray Duck ran home.

"I am not a gray duck! I am a gray goose!" he yelled.

"Good!" May Duck quacked. "I love you just the same!"

Comprehension Check

Retell

Retell the story.
Use the pictures.

Think About It

1. Why can't Gray Duck quack?
2. How is Gray Duck different from the other ducks?

Write About It

Write a letter. Tell Gray Duck why it's okay to be different.

Working with Words

Phonics

Read the words.

by	bright	day
finds	fly	high
light	night	rain
sight	stay	sky

Words to Know

Read the words.

how	does
little	many

Read the story.

A Little Bat

Bats fly at night.
How does a little bat
help us?
It eats bugs.
Bugs eat plants.
Some bugs bite us.
Bats eat many bugs.

Night Animals

by Jenny Halket

Who is up at night?
A bat is up at night.
A bat can fly.
A bat can fly high in the sky.

Many bats live in caves.
How does a bat sleep?
A bat sleeps by hanging
upside down.

A bat sleeps in the daytime.
At night, a bat wakes up.
It is time to eat.
A bat can see well at night.

A little bat can fly and fly.
This bat hunts bugs.
A bat can find many bugs in
just a night.
A bat helps us by eating bugs.

The sun is high in the sky.
It is bright.
It is hot, hot, hot!
There is not a tiger in sight.
Daytime is resting time.

At sunset, a tiger gets up.
It is not as hot at night.
It is time to hunt.

A tiger sees well at night.
It waits in the grass.

This tiger sees an animal to eat.
It runs and jumps to get it.

A tiger hunts at night.
A bat hunts at night.
At night, we rest.
But night animals are up!

Comprehension Check

Retell

Summarize the selection.
Use the pictures.

Think About It

1. Why does a tiger take its kill to a safe place?
2. Why can a bat find a lot of food at night?

Write About It

Write about a wild animal or an animal in a zoo.

Working with Words

Phonics

Read the words.

glow	go	grow
no	find	so
sky	toad	night
boat	window	road

Words to Know

Read the words.

first	soon
after	things

Read the story.

Growing Up

I will grow!
First, I am a little cub.
Soon, I will grow big.
I will look like my mom.
After I am big, I will
do so many things.

What Grows?

by Leigh Nelson

Plants Grow

Living things grow. Plants grow from seeds. First seeds go in the land.

Water helps plants grow.
After many days, plants will
grow. Drop, rain, drop!

Plants like sun. Sun helps plants grow. Sun helps plants grow big. Glow, sun, glow!

It takes time for plants to get big. Grow, plants, grow. Go, plants, go!

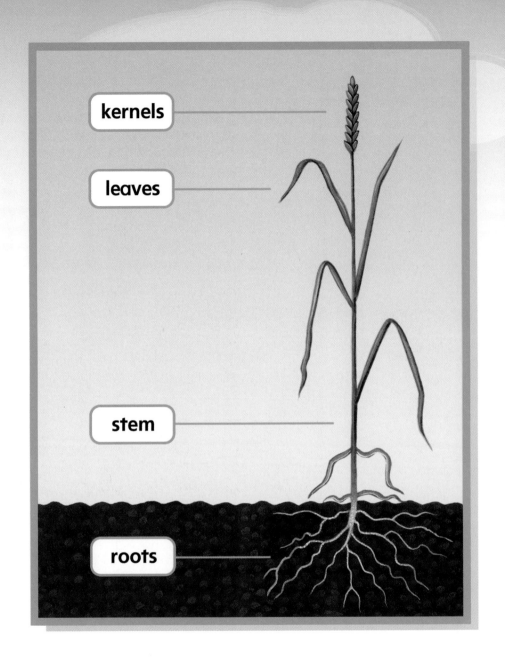

kernels

leaves

stem

roots

Soon the plants will grow
bigger. Grow, plants, grow!

Animals Grow

Some animals grow from eggs.
Toads lay eggs in the water. The
dots are toad eggs. Grow, eggs,
grow!

First, eggs grow into tadpoles.
The tadpoles will grow into
toads. Swim, tadpoles, swim!

A tadpole has no legs. Then, back legs grow. After it has legs, it is a toad. Hop, toads, hop!

Living things grow. Grow, plants, grow! Grow, toads, grow!

Comprehension Check

Retell

Summarize the selection.
Use the pictures.

Think About It

1. What can toads do after they grow legs?
2. How are plants and animals alike?

Write About It

Write about a plant or animal you know.

Working with Words

Phonics

Read the words.

be	slow	feel
dream	cold	me
meet	pea	queen
needs	sleep	sweet

Words to Know

Read the words.

put	was
know	were

Read the story.

A Good Show

We put on a show.
I did real tricks.
It was fun!
I know I did my best.
We were so good!
Mom and Dad came to
see me.

Queen Bea and the Pea

by Eileen Sherry
illustrated by Randall Enos

Who Will Be Queen?

Queen Bea was getting old.

Queen Bea said, "It is time to find a girl who will be queen after me."

Queen Bea said, "A queen needs to know if things are not right. I will meet many girls. I will make up a test to find the next queen."

The best girls in the land came. The girls were dressed in the finest dresses.

"Pick me, pick me!" the girls told Queen Bea.

Queen Bea came to a girl
named Jean. Jean did not have
a fine dress. She did not say,
"Pick me."

"Jean seems so sweet," said
Queen Bea.

Queen Bea's Plan

It was night. Queen Bea had a plan.

"I will put a pea under the beds," said Queen Bea. "The girl who can feel a pea will know if things are not right."

The girls got in bed.

Old Queen Bea said, "It is late.
Sweet dreams. Sleep well."

The girls slept well. But Jean did not sleep well.

"The bed is not right," said Jean.

The next day, old Queen Bea
asked, "Did you sleep well?"

"Yes, we slept well," said
the girls.

Jean said, "I did not sleep a
wink, my queen."

Queen Bea gave Jean a big hug.

Queen Bea said, "My sweet Jean! You felt a pea! You will be the next queen!"

Comprehension Check

Retell

Retell the story.
Use the pictures.

Think About It

1. What do the illustrations tell you about Jean?
2. Why is it important for a queen to know when things are not right?

Write About It

What do you think a good queen should be like?

Working with Words

Phonics

Read the words.

Duke	music	Lulu
Luke	meat	real
mule	see	use
tune	cute	flute

Words to Know

Read the words.

want	work
our	could

Read the story.

What I Want

I want to work.

I like to use my hands.

I helped my dad fix our truck.

I am painting a home for Duke.

I could make a lot of things.

A Talking Mule

by Leigh Nelson
illustrated by Margot Apple

Luke and Lulu had an old mule.
The mule's name was Old Gus.

Old Gus worked six days a week.
On Sundays, Old Gus rested.
On Sundays, Luke and Lulu
did not ride on Old Gus.

But on a Sunday, Luke and
Lulu had to ride.

"We must use Old Gus,"
Luke said.

Luke went to get Old Gus.

Old Gus said, "I don't work on Sunday. I rest."

"I didn't know you could talk!" Luke yelled.

Luke ran to Lulu.

"Our mule can talk!" he yelled.
"Old Gus said he won't work
on a Sunday!"

"Our mule can talk? No, it can't be," said Lulu. "Luke, you must rest. I'll get Old Gus."

Old Gus looked at Lulu.

He said, "No, I don't work on Sunday. I need to rest. And I want my hay!"

Lulu ran to Luke.

"Yes! Old Gus can talk!" yelled Lulu. "He said he won't work on Sunday!"

The cat looked up at Luke
and Lulu.

"Yes," said the cat. "And he
wants his hay!"

Comprehension Check

Retell

Retell the story.
Use the pictures.

Think About It

1. What was the big surprise in the story?
2. Why did Old Gus decide to talk on that Sunday?

Write About It

What do you think a pet would say if it could talk?

Working with Words

Phonics

Read the words.

chest	cute	she
mule	thank	that
this	when	white
chin	ship	them

Words to Know

Read the words.

small	now
give	your

Read the story.

The Small Box

My dad gave me a small box.
He said, "My dad gave me this.
Now I am a dad. I can give it
to you."
I said, "Thanks, Dad! Your old
stuff is the best."

The Old Chest

by Liane Onish
illustrated by R.W. Alley

"Let's go up to the attic,"
said Ann.

"Yes!" said Liz. "I like looking at
the old things!"

In the attic, Ann wiped dust from an old chest.

"What is in that chest?" asked Liz.

"This chest just has old
stuff in it," said Ann.

She opened the lid.

Liz looked in.
On top were paintings.

Ann said, "My paintings!
I made them when I was five!"

"That's just a pink blob,"
said Liz.

"That blob is you, Liz!" said
Ann. "I painted you when you
were a small baby!"

Liz held up a dress. It
had red and white dots on it.

"That's mine. I had it when I
was small," said Ann.

"Can I try on your dress?" Liz
asked.

Liz held up a doll.

"That's my doll!" said Ann.
"Give it to me!"

"Can I hold it?" asked Liz.

"Okay, but it's mine,"
said Ann.

Ann looked at Liz.

"You look cute in my dress," said Ann. "And you like my old doll."

Ann smiled.

She said, "That dress won't fit me now. I don't play with that doll. You can have them."

"Thanks, big sister!" said Liz.

Comprehension Check

Retell

Retell the story.
Use the pictures.

Think About It

1. What did the sisters do in this story?
2. Why do you think the girl's mom saved the old things?

Write About It

Write about something old that you have saved.

Working with Words

Phonics

Read the words.

brush	chop	crunch
crush	each	fish
inch	munch	peach
teeth	which	white

Words to Know

Read the words.

about	they
because	for

Read the story.

Brush Your Teeth!

You have about 28 teeth.
They need to be brushed.
Brush each day because you
want your teeth to last!
You will need them for a long
time!

We Need Teeth

by Nancy Ryan

Teeth help us eat. You have 3 kinds of teeth. Those in front bite and cut. The long, sharp teeth rip meat. Flat, side teeth crush and crunch things.

You can eat many things. You can eat plants like peas and peaches. You can eat meat and fish. You can eat these things because of your teeth.

A rabbit has long front teeth. It needs them for cutting plants. A rabbit does not eat meat. It just munches on plants. Its flat teeth crush them. Munch! Munch!

A cat can't munch. But its front teeth help the cat grab and hold things. Its side teeth cut these things into bits. Then the cat can eat them.

This whale eats fish, but its teeth are dull. This whale can't munch fish. Its teeth just hold them. Then the whale gulps them down.

Some animals have odd teeth. This wild pig has sharp tusks. Tusks are long, long teeth. They can be about 3-inches long. A wild pig uses its tusks when it digs for food.

This snake has sharp fangs. It uses them to bite. The snake hides. It waits for something good to eat. Then, it bites with its fangs.

This pike has sharp teeth. Some teeth go back. When a pike eats a fish, these teeth keep that fish inside. The fish can't swim away.

Teeth can be long and sharp.
Teeth can be flat. Teeth can be
dull. Teeth help animals eat.

Comprehension Check

Retell

Summarize the selection.
Use the pictures.

Think About It

1. What can a rabbit eat with its long sharp teeth?
2. Why do people have 3 kinds of teeth?

Write About It

Write about the teeth of an animal that you know.

Working with Words

Phonics

Read the words.

screech	scrap	wish
splish	scratch	spray
stray	strain	street
string	stripe	teeth

Words to Know

Read the words.

come	walk
every	any

Read the story.

Scrap Takes a Walk

"Come, Scrap!" said Jo.
"Let's walk in the rain.
I need to train you.
Don't strain on your leash!"
Every street was wet.
Jo did not see any dry spots.
Splish! Splash! went the pals.

The Stray Dog

by Nicole Lyle
illustrated by Nancy Cote

Let's Get a Pet!

Ray skipped down the street.
He was getting a pet!

"Come on, Dad," he said. "Walk
faster! There won't be any good
pets left."

"What kind of pet will we get?"
Dad asked.

"The best kind," said Ray.

Then Ray looked up the street.
A big yellow dog wagged its tail.

He ran to the dog. It licked
his hand.

"This dog likes me!" he said.

"That is a stray dog," Dad told
Ray. "Scram!"

But the dog did not scram.
It sat still. It held up its paw.

"Dad!" said Ray. "This dog can
shake hands!"

"Come on," said Dad. "We will
find a better pet in the shop."

The Best Pet

In the shop, Ray looked at the pets. A cat was playing with string.

"Cats are cute and sit on your lap," said Dad.

"But I want a pet I can take for walks," said Ray.

"Pick me!" came a screech.

"That bird can speak," said the pet shop man. "You put seeds on its tray to feed it."

"But I want a pet that can play catch," said Ray.

Ray came to the dogs. He
played with a big dog and a
little dog. He played with a
spotted dog. He played with
a striped dog. He played with
every dog.

"Ruff! Ruff!"

Ray looked up.

It was the big yellow dog!

"Dad!" he said. "That stray dog has no home. Can he be my pet? I like him best."

"We need to get him checked," said Dad.

Ray and Dad went to the vet.
The vet checked the stray dog.

"He's fine!" the vet said.
"He will be a good pet."

Ray hugged the stray dog.
He had the best pet!

Comprehension Check

Retell

Retell the story.
Use the pictures.

Think About It

1. What different kinds of dogs did Ray see at the pet shop?
2. Why do you think Ray didn't find a dog he wanted in the pet shop?

Write About It

Write about a pet you have or would like to have.

Working with Words

Phonics

Read the words.

car	dark	dart
far	street	mark
Mars	park	star
start	hard	stripe

Words to Know

Read the words.

race	found
funny	along

Read the story.

Race to Mars!

Let's hop in a ship and race to Mars. Mars is far away. It looks like a red star. When we have found Mars, we will get off. I hope we find something funny there! Come along and we will see.

A Funny Trip to Mars

by Carolina Su
illustrated by Julia Gorton

Liz and Clark found a flying car!

"Let's take a trip!" said Liz.

"Let's go far away," said Clark.
"Let's go to Mars!"

Liz and Clark drove fast.

"Which way is Mars?" Liz asked.

"I think it's that way," said
Clark. "Come along!"

Cars darted past. Drivers waved
at Liz and Clark.

"Flying elephants and frogs!
That's funny!" said Clark.

The dark sky started filling up
with cars, trucks, and buses. It
was hard to drive.

A car with dogs darted past.
The dogs gave a big bark!

Liz said, "I think it's a race."

Clark said, "If it is, we are last!
Let's go faster!"

A bus zipped by.

"We can win!" said Liz.

Liz and Clark drove hard and fast. They passed every car.

"I see Mars!" said Liz.

"We must land on it to win,"
said Clark.

"Look at that!" said Liz.

Liz and Clark could not park on Mars.

"We can't end this race!" said Clark.

"But we can *start* a race," said Liz. "Let's go back home!"

On your mark, get set, GO! And off they went.

Comprehension Check

Retell

Retell the story.
Use the pictures.

Think About It

1. Why couldn't Liz and Clark land on Mars?
2. What makes the ending funny?

Write About It

Write about where you would go if you had a flying car.

Working with Words

Read the words.

dark	born	before
for	form	hard
or	storm	shore
short	start	more

Read the words.

blue	fall
very	full

Read the poem.

A Short Storm

The sky is blue.
The day is warm.
The shore is dry.
Here comes a storm!
The raindrops fall
so very fast!
The lake is full.
The storm has passed!

Storms, Storms!

by Holly Melton

Before a storm, the sky can be clear and blue. But clouds can form, and fill with water.

When clouds are as full as can be, rain falls. Rainstorms can last for a short or long time.

When it is very cold, snow can fall. After a snowstorm, the digging begins!

This kind of storm happens when it is so cold that rain freezes. Tree branches snap. The streets are like skating rinks!

CRASH! CLAP! goes the thunder. Thunderstorms can make strong winds.

Big forks of lightning may come from the sky! Lightning can scorch trees and start fires on land.

A big thunderstorm can make
a lot of wind. When strong
winds blow and twist, they
can form into a big cloud with
a tail. A twister is born.

You can see big storms from up high in a plane. The sea is under these blowing and twisting winds. This storm is about to reach land.

The storm has reached the shore. When this kind of storm hits the coast, it can be bad for homes, stores, and trees.

This is a very odd kind of storm. There is no rain or snow or thunder or lightning. But there is wind.

The wind is so strong that it picks up sand and blows it into big clouds. It is hard to see in a sandstorm!

Comprehension Check

Retell

Summarize the selection.
Use the pictures.

Think About It

1. What are twisters like?
2. Which kinds of storms happen where you live?

 Write About It

Write about one kind of storm you know.

Working with Words

Phonics

Read the words.

Bert	dirt	Fern
first	for	girl
more	her	shirt
third	torn	bird

Words to Know

Read the words.

never	been
one	together

Read the story.

First Time at Bat

Bert had never been in a game before. He was at bat. He got one strike. Then he had a hit! He ran to third base.

"Keep going!" His teammates yelled together.

Bert did. It was a home run!

Fern's Team

by Mark Majuk
illustrated by Kathryn Mitter

Fern was a girl who liked to play baseball.

One day, Fern went for a walk. She had her mitt with her.

Fern saw some boys playing
baseball.

A boy said, "Hi! Will you play
with us?"

"Yes!" said Fern.

The boys did not know that Fern
was a girl.

The boy asked Fern to play third base. Fern had a strong arm. She threw far.

She played well. One time, she had to dive for the ball.

Fern got it! Her shirt was torn.
She had dirt on her.

The boys on her team spoke
together.

"That kid can catch!" they said.
"But can he hit?"

Fern had been up at bat many
times. But she had not played
with this team before.

Fern's team needed a run to win. The ball came. Fern let it go.

BALL ONE!

The ball came. Fern missed it.

STRIKE ONE!

The ball came. Fern did not miss it this time!

CRACK!!!

The ball sailed a long, long way.

HOME RUN!

"Yay!" cried the team.

"My name's Fern," said Fern.
And off came her hat!

"You're a girl!" said a boy. "We
never had a girl on the team!"

"But you can be the first!" said a boy. "You helped us win. Fern, please stay on the team!"

"Okay," Fern smiled. And she did.

Comprehension Check

Retell

Retell the story.
Use the pictures.

Think About It

1. What did you think the boys would do when they found out Fern was a girl?
2. Why do you think Fern didn't say that she was a girl?

Write About It

Write about a game you like to play.

Working with Words

Phonics

Read the words.

bird	blur	curl
first	fur	her
hurt	purple	spurt
turn	turtle	urchin

Words to Know

Read the words.

all	wash
over	brown

Read the story.

The Sea Urchin

Look at all the sharp purple spines on this sea urchin! They look like they could hurt! The spines keep them safe.

Sea urchins stick on rocks and let the sea wash over them. They feed on brown seaweed.

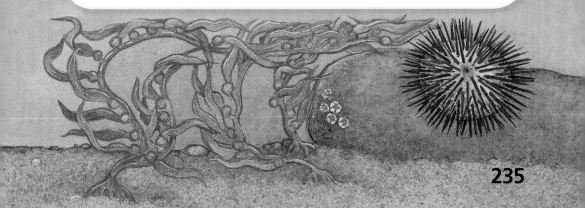

Fur, Skin, and Scales

by Felipe Sanchez

What's on the outside of an animal?

Frogs have skin. A frog breathes with its lungs and skin! Its skin must stay wet, so frogs let water wash over them.

This animal must be in the water all the time. If it is mad, its skin turns from brown to red! If it is not safe, it spurts dark ink. Then it can't be seen.

This animal has sharp spines.
When it's not safe, it curls up.
Its spines can hurt, so foxes
looking for a meal stay away!

Fur is on the outside of many animals. It keeps them warm. Fur helps this big cat blend in with rocks, trees, and grasses.

This big cat can purr. It is cute, but don't get close!

In the winter, this rabbit's fur turns white. This keeps it safe. Animals can't see the white rabbit in the snow, so they can't catch it!

What's on the outside of a snake? Skin and scales!

This snake's skin is old and worn. So the snake will get rid of it. After it's finished, the snake will look fresh.

Where is the rest of this turtle? It is inside the shell! A turtle's shell keeps its soft parts safe from animals like skunks, foxes, and snakes.

And what's on the outside of a bird?

Here's a hint! These things help birds keep warm and... fly!

Animal	Covering
Rabbit	Fur
Giraffe	Fur
Hedgehog	Spines
Porcupine	Spines
Turtle	Shell
Snail	Shell

Think of an animal. What is on the outside of it? Is it fur, skin, scales, spines, or a shell?

Comprehension Check

Retell

Summarize the selection.
Use the pictures.

Think About It

1. How do fur, skin, scales, and
   shells on the outside of
   animals help them?
2. How is an egg shell different
   from a turtle shell?

Write About It

Write about the outside of
an animal you know.

Working with Words

Phonics

Read the words.

cook	curl	fur
good	hook	hurt
look	nook	stood
took	wood	wool

Words to Know

Read the words.

here	year
people	young

Read the story.

Egg Farm

Here at the farm, hens lay eggs all year. The farmer will sell some of the eggs. People like to cook and eat eggs.

The farmer will not sell all the eggs. Some of them will hatch. Young chicks will be born.

From Sheep to Wool

by Lenika Gael
illustrated by Michael Hobbs

Wool helps people stay warm.

On freezing days, we can put on wool coats, hats, and scarves. We get wool from sheep. Wool is the name for a sheep's fur.

A sheep ranch is a kind of farm. At
a sheep ranch, ranchers try hard to
keep the sheep safe and well.

A lamb is a young sheep. At a sheep ranch, lots of cute lambs are born each year.

This lamb stays close by his mom. She will feed and clean him.

The sheep roam on top of high hills. They look for good, fresh grass to eat.

If the grass is good, the sheep stay. If it is not, the sheep leave to look for better grass.

If the sheep stray too far, sheep dogs can find them. Smart sheep dogs can find sheep in any nook. Sheep dogs help by leading the sheep home.

In winter, a sheep needs its thick wool to keep warm. But in summer it is hot, and sheep do not need much wool.

This sheep is having his wool cut. The cutting does not hurt the sheep. His good, thick wool will be used to make things that keep people warm in winter.

Sheep ranchers sell wool to mills. At a mill, wool is spun into yarn. Yarn can be made into a lot of things, such as hats and scarves.

Here is a coat made of wool. If you see a wool coat or scarf, think of sheep at a ranch. That's where the wool came from.

Comprehension Check

Retell

Summarize the selection.
Use the pictures.

Think About It

1. What did the author want you to learn from reading this selection?
2. How do the animals in the selection help people?

Write About It

Write about some other things that animals give us.

Working with Words

Phonics

Read the words.

chew	flew	fruit
good	scoop	loose
mood	new	soon
too	tooth	wood

Words to Know

Read the words.

would	around
pull	out

Read the story.

A New Nest

"Would you help me make a new nest?" Red Bird asked.

Blue Bird nodded. The birds flew around to find things to use. Red Bird can pull twigs out of the dirt. Blue Bird can scoop up some mud. Soon Red Bird had a new nest.

259

The Loose Tooth

by Rachel Mann
illustrated by Jeff Hopkins

Little Rabbit had a loose tooth.

He wiggled it. He jiggled it. He tapped it. But the tooth would not come out.

Then Mouse came by.

"I will help," he said. "I will put a string around the tooth. Then I will pull as hard as I can."

"No, thanks," said Little Rabbit. "That would hurt too much!"

Little Rabbit wiggled the tooth. But the tooth did not come out.

He was not in a good mood. He wanted his loose tooth to come out soon.

Then Squirrel came by.

"I will help," she said. "If you chew on this wood, your tooth will come out."

"No, thanks," said Little Rabbit. "I will not chew on wood. I like to chew on fruit."

Then Dog came by.

"I will help," said Dog. "I will use this hammer to tap on the tooth. A hammer can get that tooth out."

"No, thanks," said Little Rabbit. "I do not want a hammer tapping on my tooth."

He wiggled his tooth some more. But it still would not come out!

Little Rabbit went back home. His friends came, too. "We can help!" they yelled.

"Use a string!" yelled Mouse.

"Chew on wood!" yelled Squirrel.

"Try a hammer!" yelled Dog.

"No, thanks!" said Little Rabbit.

He wiggled his tooth. He jiggled it.
He tapped it and pulled it . . .

. . . AND AT LAST IT CAME OUT!

Little Rabbit hugged his friends. He said, "Thanks so much for your help!"

Then he went to show his mom and dad the tooth.

Comprehension Check

Retell

Retell the story.
Use the pictures.

Think About It

1. What is Little Rabbit's problem?
   How does he solve the problem?
2. Do you think Little Rabbit's friends
   helped him solve his problem?
   Explain.

Write About It

Write about a time when you
had a loose tooth.

Working with Words

Phonics

Read the words.

chew	fruit	scratch
scruff	soon	splash
spring	sprint	street
stretch	string	stripe

Words to Know

Read the words.

two	seven
eight	learn

Read the story.

See Puppies Grow!

The two puppies are seven weeks old. They like to chew and scratch things. They stretch and rest.

At eight weeks, the puppies can sprint and chase. They learn many new things. They are growing up fast!

All About Kittens

by Lenika Gael

illustrated by Kristen Goeters

Look at the kittens! They were just born. They are very little and very cute.

Kittens can't see at first. But they don't have to go far for food. Mom Cat gives them her warm milk.

Mom Cat picks up each kitten by the scruff of its neck. She puts them in a safe spot. This does not hurt the kittens.

Soon the kittens are one week old. They can see!

At two weeks old, Mom Cat cleans her kittens. She licks them. She teaches each kitten to clean its fur.

At three weeks old, the kittens
learn to walk. It is hard at first.
The kittens fall, but they don't
mind. They get up and keep trying.

At four weeks old, the kittens start
to play. They run and jump. They
bite and scratch. The kittens have a
good time!

At five weeks old, the kittens can
lick food from a plate. They can
clean themselves, too. Mom Cat
showed them how.

At six weeks old, the kittens don't
need to be with Mom Cat all the
time. They can eat, play, and sleep
by themselves. The kittens are
growing up!

At seven weeks old, the kittens can
go up steps. They like to play with
string. They sprint and run and play
all day. Then they stretch and take
a rest.

At eight weeks old, the kittens are getting new teeth. They can eat hard food. Soon they will be cats.

Cats are nice pets. What pet do you like best?

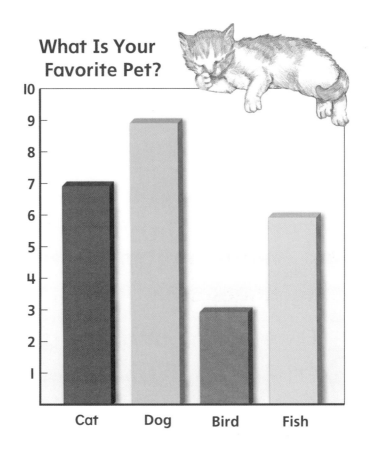

What Is Your Favorite Pet?

Comprehension Check

Retell

Summarize the selection.
Use the pictures.

Think About It

1. What is this selection mainly about? What details did you learn?
2. What are three ways that Mom Cat takes care of her kittens?

Write About It

Write about a baby pet. Tell how it changes as it grows.

Working with Words

Phonics

Read the words.

awful	draw	fault
flaw	law	Paul
scratch	straw	Dawn
string	lawn	saw

Words to Know

Read the words.

school	write
buy	laugh

Read the story.

The School Sale

The school was having a sale. But Dawn did not have anything to sell. She felt awful.

"I know," she said. "I can sell jokes. I will write them down."

Many kids came to buy jokes. Kids like to laugh!

Jokes for Sale

283

Paul's School Trip

A Rhyme by Rachel Mann
illustrated by Betina Ogden

Paul's day started out well.
School trip day! Yes!
But how did a zoo trip
end up in such a mess?

First Paul saw zebras.
They were striped black and white.
He said, "They look boring.
I'll make them look right!"

Paul started to draw
green dots and red.
He drew on the zebras.
Then Teacher shook his head.

"You can't write on zebras!
This zoo has laws!
Go sit on that bench —
and work on your flaws!"

Paul then sat sadly
under a tree.
The rest of the zoo,
he so wished to see.

"What can I do as
the day passes by?
There's nothing to read.
There's nothing to buy."

To make the time pass,
Paul ate his food.
He said, "I feel awful.
I'm in a bad mood."

Just then a big bird
flew by Paul's seat.
It came very close.
It wanted to eat!

"Real wildlife!" said Paul.
"This is so neat!"
He gave it a snack.
The bird liked the treat.

The bird said to Paul,
"Would you like to fly?"
Paul jumped on its wing.
They flew to the sky!

"I'm having such fun!"
Paul laughed with glee.
"Trips to the zoo are
as fun as can be."

Then the zookeeper saw
the big bird with Paul.
Her look said that she
was not glad at all.

"I saw that ride and
safe it was not!
Kids in the zoo must
stay in a safe spot."

"It isn't my fault!"
Paul said to her.
"The bird picked me up.
It was a big blur."

"I'm glad you are fine.
Let's go find your class.
I see them right there,
standing next to the glass."

Paul looked that way.
He saw them, too.
The rest of the day,
Paul had fun at the zoo.

Comprehension Check

Retell

Retell the story.
Use the pictures.

Think About It

1. What happened to Paul after he drew on the zebras?
2. How is Paul's trip to the zoo awful? How is it also good?

Write About It

Write about a school trip that you went on.

Working with Words

Phonics

Read the words.

down	fault	ground
flower	wow	now
ouch	out	round
shout	saw	found

Words to Know

Read the words.

pretty	color
other	call

Read the story.

What Is It?

This pretty flower comes in lots of colors. Some grow on thick shrubs. Others have long stems. If you grab it, you may shout, "Ouch!" It has thorns.

What do we call that flower? A rose.

Flower Garden

by B. R. Shah

Flowers from Seeds

Do you like flowers? If you do, you can plant a flower garden outside.

First find a good spot. The flowers will need dirt, sun, and rain. Then choose which flowers to plant.

Some flowers grow from seeds.
The seeds are planted under the
ground. Then the seeds grow into
new plants.

Sunflowers grow from seeds. A sunflower has big yellow flowers and green leaves. It needs a lot of sun to grow. It is called a sunflower because it turns to the sun.

Sunflowers can grow very big. Some grow ten feet high!

Forget-me-nots grow from seeds.
Forget-me-nots are little blue
flowers. They have short green
stems and little leaves.

Forget-me-nots bloom in the spring.
They grow best in light shade.

Flowers from Bulbs

Some flowers grow from bulbs. Bulbs are round and grow under the ground. They are planted in holes in the dirt.

Snowdrops grow from bulbs. Snowdrops are little white flowers. The flowers droop upside down from short stems.

Snowdrop bulbs must be planted in the fall. The bulbs grow into little plants, and the flowers bloom in the winter.

Tulips grow from bulbs. Tulips
bloom in the spring. They come in
many pretty colors. Most tulips are
shaped like bells or bowls.

Daffodils grow from bulbs. They are fine flowers for a spring garden. The flower has a narrow part shaped like a cup.

Daffodils are not hard to grow. They can grow and bloom in full sun or light shade.

Flowers come in any color of the rainbow. Some are big and bold. Others are little and sweet. Flowers can grow in the sun or shade.

Go get some seeds or bulbs. Plant a flower garden and see the flowers bloom!

Comprehension Check

Retell

Summarize the selection.
Use the pictures.

Think About It

1. Which kinds of flowers grow from seeds? Which grow from bulbs?
2. Which flowers like the cold?

Write About It

Plan your own flower garden.
What flowers would you plant?

Working with Words

Phonics

Read the words.

boy	coin	cow
Joy	noise	oil
join	point	Roy
shout	toy	Troy

Words to Know

Read the words.

heard	again
should	door

Read the story.

What Troy Heard

Troy Pig heard a tapping noise.
He did not like that noise one bit.
Troy heard it again.

"Should we lock the door?"
he asked Mom Pig.

Mom smiled. She pointed.
"You heard a bird pecking
at a tree!"

Roy and Joy

by Lilly Chin
illustrated by Mark Corcoran

Roy and Joy were high up in a tree.
They saw a big house.

"Should we go in?" asked Roy.

"Why not?" said Joy. "We are brave! We will look for toys."

Roy pointed to the window.

"You first," he said.

"No, no, after you," said Joy.

Roy and Joy went in.

"Help!" yelled Roy. "That's a boy. He is looking right at me."

"That is not a real boy!" said Joy. "Be brave, Roy."

"Let's look in that trunk," said Roy.
"Toys might be inside."

"You first," said Joy.
Roy opened the trunk. "I see a coin,
but no toys," he said.

"I heard a noise!" Joy said.

"That's the trunk lid creaking," said
Roy. "It needs to be oiled."

They found a box. It had long, thin blocks in it.

"These look like bones!" said Roy.

"Maybe we should stay away from them," said Joy.

Then they found a door.

"Look at this! I think toys might be in there," said Roy. "Let's go in and look."

"You go first!" said Joy.

"Help!" yelled Roy. "Look, Joy! There are bears in here. Let's get out fast!"

"Me first!" shouted Joy.

Roy and Joy ran out to the tree.

"That was close!" said Joy. "And we didn't find any toys!"

Roy pointed to the window.

"Let's not go there again," he said.

"Well," said Joy. "It's a good thing we are both so brave!"

"That's right!" said Roy.

Comprehension Check

Retell

Retell the story.
Use the pictures.

Think About It

1. How are Roy and Joy like real raccoons? How are they different?
2. Do you think Roy feels brave at the end of the story? Why or why not?

Write About It

Write about a time when you felt brave.

Working with Words

Phonics

Read the words.

knee	knight	wrist
wreck	knock	toy
knit	noise	knot
wrap	write	wrote

Words to Know

Read the words.

always	family
thought	idea

Read the story.

A Family Birthday

Hi Gramps,

It is Mom's birthday. I always like family birthdays! Dad and I thought about a gift. Then I had an idea! Here are some hints. It can sit on Mom's knee. We can't wrap it. It's cute. Write back!

Miss you,

Ron

Dear Pen Pal

by Lucy Floyd
illustrated by Amy Huntington

Dear Tran,

I'm so glad we're pen pals. I'll write to you lots. I'm the new kid in town. School is out, so it's hard to make new friends.

This is a snapshot of my family and me. Mom likes to knit!

Your pen pal,
Meg

Dear Meg,

I like being your pen pal. This is a snapshot of my family and me.

I was sad when my family first came here. But now I have lots of friends. You will, too!

Your pen pal,
Tran

Hi Tran,

Thanks for telling me you made new friends. I hope I will, too!

This is a snapshot of Ms. Wright and me. She's a teacher I had last year.

So long,
Meg

Dear Meg,

When I was the new kid in town,
I joined things. I liked the swim
team a lot.

Are there kids on your block?
That's always a good start.

Until next time,
Tran

Greetings Tran,

Good news! There's a boy right next door. His name is Sam. We rode our bikes and had fun. I took this snapshot of him. I think I have a new friend!

Hopefully,
Meg

Greetings Meg,

I'm glad you wrote that you have
a new friend. I thought you would!

I am in a play now. You always meet
kids in plays. I am a knight.

So long for now,
Tran

Hi Tran,

Bad news! I haven't seen Sam for five days! I thought we had a very good time. But he must not like me.

Sadly,
Meg

Hi Meg,

I feel bad that Sam isn't acting like a friend.

I fell and sprained my wrist and foot. Dad had to wrap me up in that white stuff. I can't go out and play for a week!

Best,
Tran

Dear Tran,

You gave me an idea! I went to Sam's house and knocked on the door. His mom said Sam hurt his knee and had to stay in. So I went in and played games with him. He was so glad to see me!

Your pen pal friend,
Meg

Comprehension Check

Retell

Retell the story.
Use the pictures.

Think About It

1. Why did Meg wait five days to check on Sam?
2. How did Tran help Meg make friends?

Write About It

Write a letter to a pen pal you would like to have.

Working with Words

Phonics

Read the words.

age	wrap	knock
huge	knock	page
place	race	space
cent	write	nice

Words to Know

Read the words.

air	carry
Earth	move

Read the story.

Stars in Space

Have you walked in the night air and looked at stars? It might be nice to pluck one and carry it home!

Stars look little, but they are huge. The Sun is a star. It gives our Earth light and heat. Stars move in space. Can you see them?

IN SPACE

by JOHN STAFFORD

People in past ages looked at the sun, stars, and planets. They looked up at the face of the moon. Back then, people dreamed that they might fly into space. Now, that dream is real!

Astronaut Buzz Aldrin walks on the moon.

Astronauts first landed on the moon in 1969. They placed a flag on the moon. When they returned to Earth, they had moon rocks.

Spacecrafts carry astronauts into space. Rockets fire, and the spacecraft is on its way!

Crews on the spacecrafts have many jobs. They find out if people can live in space for a long time. They perform tests and keep records. These are sent back to Earth.

On Earth, gravity keeps us from floating up in the air. In space, there is no gravity. Crews float when they move from place to place.

Food needs to be in bags that are tied down so it will not float. When astronauts sleep, straps keep them from floating.

Astronauts can go outside a spacecraft. This page shows them on a space walk. A cord keeps them from floating off!

Some astronauts work in a space lab. This shows Skylab. A lab has more room than a spacecraft. Crews can stay in space longer. They can look at the Earth from space and send back facts.

Sojourner robot/rover explores Mars.

Space probes can go into space without people. A probe can send back facts about a planet. The probe on this page went to Mars. Can people live on Mars? Probes tell us a lot about this.

Huge telescopes like this show us stars in space. What is a star made of? How far away is it? A telescope helps tell us these things and more.

International Space Station

Our race to space goes on. We will find out more and more about space. Those dreamers from the past would be glad!

Comprehension Check

Retell

Summarize the selection.
Use the pictures.

Think About It

1. Do you think exploring space is a
   good idea? Support your answer.
2. Why do you think the author
   wrote about space?

Write About It

What do you think astronauts
will find out next in space?

Working with Words

Phonics

Read the words.

barge	bridge	change
face	badge	huge
judge	large	range
sludge	space	strange

Words to Know

Read the words

through	done
world	built

Read the story.

Bridges, Old and New

In the past, not all bridges were large. Many of them were like little tunnels. People went through them! The roof and sides kept the bridge dry in the rain. Now things have changed. What is done in today's world? Bridges are built of steel.

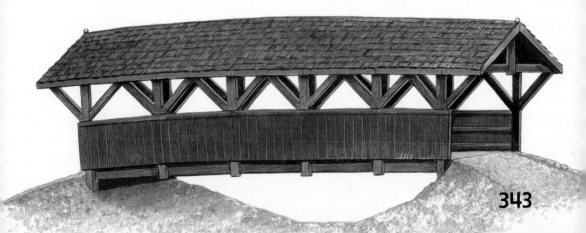

Bridges And Tunnels

by Lucy McClymont

Bridges Help Us

This bridge is in Japan. It is the longest bridge in the world.

The bridge hangs from strong wires that are held down at each end. Like many other bridges, it is grand and it is useful.

This is a beam bridge.
Large beams rest on
a base below. The
center part is called a
drawbridge. It lifts to
let boats go through.

Sailboats pass under this
drawbridge in Chicago.

The arch bridge gets its name from its shape.

This bridge is an arch bridge. In the past, arch bridges were built of stone. Today, that has changed. Now arch bridges can be built of concrete and steel.

This is a pontoon bridge. The center parts float. The pontoons are linked to land by short bridges. Why was this strange bridge built? The lake bed has mud and sludge in it. Other kinds of bridges couldn't be built in mud.

This is the widest floating bridge in the world.

This is one of the highest footbridges in the world.

We need bridges to cross lakes and rivers. They must be strong for cars and trucks. But some bridges are for feet! This footbridge is between two towers!

Tunnels Link Places

There are tunnels below roads. Tunnels go through hills and under rivers. Tunnels help us go places we want to go!

Cars, trains, and trucks travel through tunnels.

The Channel Tunnel includes three tunnels.

Some tunnels are below the sea. This one is the Channel Tunnel. It was built under the channel linking England and France. Way down under the sea, rocks and clay were dug out. When the tunnel was done, railroad tracks were put in.

The Channel Tunnel has a nickname. It's called a "Chunnel"! People ride high-speed trains through the Chunnel.

This is the fastest train in the world.

Some tunnels are high up on hills. Some are in towns. Tunnels go all through the world. They help make our trips faster and safer.

Are tunnels and bridges a good thing? You be the judge!

This tunnel goes through a hill.

Comprehension Check

Retell

Summarize the selection.
Use the pictures.

Think About It

1. How are bridges and tunnels
   different? How are they alike?
2. How would the way people travel
   be different if there were no
   bridges or tunnels?

Write About It

Write about a bridge you know.
Tell what it looks like.

Working with Words

Phonics

Read the words.

hair	bridge	chair
dare	fair	hare
mare	bear	pear
stare	strange	square

Words to Know

Read the words.

once	upon
picture	only

Read the story.

Bear's Bad Day

Once upon a time, Bear had a very bad day. He woke up late. When he sat down to eat, a picture fell on him. Not a thing went right!

"Do I dare try anything more?" said Bear. "No, there's only one thing to do. I'll just sit right here on this chair!"

The Art Fair

by Sarah Sams
illustrated by
Pamela Harrelson

Once upon a time, there was
going to be an art fair.

Hare went to town.
She blew her horn.

"In two weeks we will
have an Art and Craft
Fair!" yelled Hare.

"What will I make for the fair?" Hare asked herself.

She looked at Goat's rug.

"That's nice, Goat," said Hare. "I'll draw a picture of it. Maybe that will give me an idea."

Hare hopped home and
hung her picture. Then she
sat in a chair and stared
at it.

"Now I'll get an idea,"
said Hare. But she didn't.

Hare went to see Mare. She was dying hair ribbons.

"What a good idea for the art fair!" said Hare.

She drew a picture of it.

"I will hang up my picture. It will help me think of an idea," said Hare.

Now, there was only one day left until the fair. Hare still did not have an idea.

She blew her horn to help her think.

"Stop it, Hare!" everyone yelled. "We are working."

So Hare looked at what
everyone was making.

She drew a picture of each
thing to help her think. She
drew a ribbon. She drew a
drum. She drew a bowl.

Hare hopped home. She
hung up her pictures. She
stared at them for a long
time.

"Now I know what I'll make
for the fair!" she cried.

Hare started cutting out her pictures. Then she stitched the squares onto cloth. She was careful as she stitched.

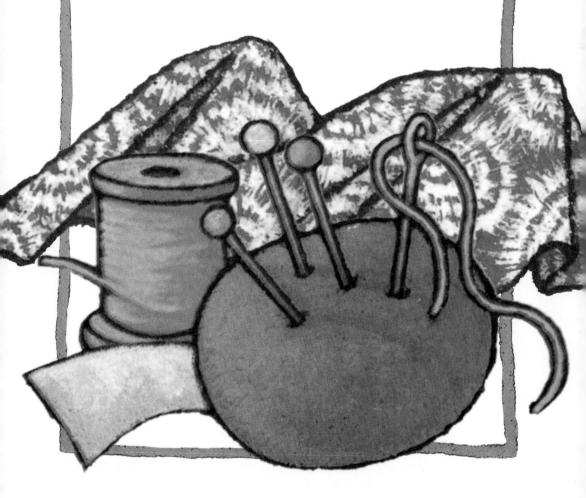

What did Hare make for the fair?

A quilt! All of her pictures were on the quilt.

"What a good idea I had!" said Hare.

Comprehension Check

Retell

Retell the story.
Use the pictures.

Think About It

1. How is Hare different from the other characters in the story?
2. Do you think Hare enjoyed making her craft for the fair? Why or why not?

Write About It

Write about something special you have made.

Skills and Strategies

TITLE	PHONICS	HIGH-FREQUENCY WORDS	COMPREHENSION
Unit 1 pages 6–65			
6 The Hat	/a/a b<u>a</u>t, /i/i b<u>i</u>g	look she the who	Analyze Story Structure: Characters and Setting
18 Yum! Yum!	/o/o m<u>o</u>p, /e/e h<u>e</u>n, /u/u m<u>u</u>g	help said you eat	Analyze Story Structure: Plot
30 Frogs, Frogs, Frogs!	initial consonant blends: *l*-blends, *s*-blends, *r*-blends	some this what do	Summarize: Main Idea and Details
42 Kids Can Make It!	/a/a h<u>a</u>t, /ā/a_e c<u>a</u>k<u>e</u>	with see and he	Summarize: Main Idea and Details
54 Pig on His Bike	/i/i p<u>i</u>g, /ī/i_e b<u>i</u>k<u>e</u>	of down to yellow	Summarize: Make and Confirm Predictions
Unit 2 pages 66–125			
66 Animal Homes	/o/o h<u>o</u>p, /ō/o_e h<u>o</u>m<u>e</u>	where under live warm	Summarize: Draw Conclusions
78 A Home Made Band	/u/u fun, /ū/u_e c<u>u</u>b<u>e</u>, fl<u>u</u>t<u>e</u>	have show play we	Summarize: Sequence
90 Who Is Best?	consonant blends: initial, medial, final	from there are before	Summarize: Sequence
102 The Gray Duck	/ā/ai pl<u>ai</u>n, ay pl<u>ay</u>	my away good four	Generate Questions: Make Inferences
114 Night Animals	/ī/i w<u>i</u>ld, igh br<u>igh</u>t, y b<u>y</u>	how does little many	Generate Questions: Make Inferences
Unit 3 pages 126–185			
126 What Grows?	/ō/oa b<u>oa</u>t, o n<u>o</u>, ow gr<u>ow</u>	after things first soon	Monitor Comprehension: Cause and Effect
138 Queen Bea and the Pea	/ē/e b<u>e</u>, ee m<u>ee</u>t, ea dr<u>ea</u>m	put were was know	Monitor Comprehension: Use Illustrations
150 A Talking Mule	/ū/u_e c<u>u</u>t<u>e</u>, u men<u>u</u>	want work our could	Visualize: Summarize
162 The Old Chest	/ch/ch <u>ch</u>est, /sh/sh <u>sh</u>ell, /th/th <u>th</u>is, /hw/wh <u>wh</u>ite	small now give your	Visualize: Cause and Effect
174 We Need Teeth	/sh/sh br<u>sh</u>, /ch/ch ea<u>ch</u>, /th/th tee<u>th</u>	about because for they	Visualize: Cause and Effect

TITLE	PHONICS	HIGH-FREQUENCY WORDS	COMPREHENSION
Unit 4 pages 186–245			
186 The Stray Dog	/skr/*scr* s<u>cr</u>ap, /spl/*spl* s<u>pl</u>ash, /spr/*spr* s<u>pr</u>ay, /str/*str* s<u>tr</u>ay	any come every walk	Generate Questions: Compare and Contrast
198 A Funny Trip to Mars	/är/*ar* c<u>ar</u>	found funny along race	Generate Questions: Cause and Effect
210 Storms, Storms!	/ôr/*or* f<u>or</u>k, *ore* sh<u>ore</u>	blue fall full very	Generate Questions: Description
222 Fern's Team	/ûr/*ir* f<u>ir</u>st, *er* h<u>er</u>	been never one together	Monitor Comprehension: Make and Confirm Predictions
234 Fur, Skin, and Scales	/ûr/*ur* f<u>ur</u>	all brown over wash	Monitor Comprehension: Make Inferences
Unit 5 pages 246–305			
246 From Sheep to Wool	/ů/*oo* c<u>oo</u>k	here people year young	Summarize: Author's Purpose
258 The Loose Tooth	/ü/*oo* t<u>oo</u>th	around out pull would	Visualize: Problem and Solution
270 All About Kittens	/skr/*scr* s<u>cr</u>atch, /spl/*spl* s<u>pl</u>ash, /spr/*spr* s<u>pr</u>ing, /str/*str* s<u>tr</u>eet	eight learn seven two	Summarize: Main Idea and Details
282 Paul's School Trip	/ô/*au* f<u>au</u>lt, *aw* dr<u>aw</u>	buy laugh school write	Summarize: Sequence
294 Flower Garden	/ou/*ow* d<u>ow</u>n, *ou* gr<u>ou</u>nd	call color other pretty	Summarize: Classify and Categorize
Unit 6 pages 306–365			
306 Roy and Joy	/oi/*oi* c<u>oi</u>n, *oy* b<u>oy</u>	again door heard should	Analyze Story Structure: Fantasy and Reality
318 Dear Pen Pal	/n/*kn* <u>kn</u>it, /r/*wr* <u>wr</u>ite	always family idea thought	Analyze Text Structure: Draw Conclusions
330 In Space	/j/*g* a<u>g</u>e, /s/*c* ra<u>c</u>e	air carry Earth move	Analyze Text Structure: Make Judgments
342 Bridges and Tunnels	endings: -ge, -dge, -rge, -nge	built done through world	Monitor Comprehension: Compare and Contrast
354 The Art Fair	/âr/*air* h<u>air</u>, *are* c<u>are</u>, *ear* b<u>ear</u>	once only picture upon	Monitor Comprehension: Character and Setting

ACKNOWLEDGMENTS

ILLUSTRATIONS

7-16: Diane Palmisciano. 19-28: Erin Mauterer. 31: Deborah Melmon. 43: Rachel Farquharson. 44-52: Annette Cable. 55: Rachel Farquharson. 56-64: Richard Bernal. 67: Barry Rockwell. 79-88: Cary Pillo. 91-100: Deborah Melmon. 103: Cary Pillo. 104-112: José Cruz. 115: Barry Rockwell. 127: Carol Schwartz. 139: Karen Dugan. 140-148: Randall Enos. 151-160: Margot Apple. 163-172: R.W. Alley. 175: Cary Pillo. 187: Melissa Iwai. 188-196: Nancy Cote. 199: Melissa Iwai. 200-208: Julia Gorton. 211: Rachel Farquharson. 223-232: Kathryn Mitter. 235: Ka Botzis. 247: Jill Newton. 248-256: Michael Hobbs. 259: Jacqueline Decker. 260-268: Jeff Hopkins. 271: Sarah Dillard. 272-280: Kristen Goeters. 283: Barry Ablett. 284-292: Betina Ogden. 295: Jacqueline Decker. 307: Aleksey Ivanov. 308-316: Mark Corcoran. 319: Elizabeth Wolf. 320-328: Amy Huntington. 331: Ruth Flanigan. 343: Doug Knutson. 355: Aleksey Ivanov. 356-364: Pam-ela Harrelson.

PHOTOGRAPHY

All photographs are by Macmillan/McGraw Hill (MMH) except as noted below:

3: Janet Foster/Masterfile; 4: Dacorum Gold/Alamy; 5: Digital Vision/SuperStock; 32: Janet Foster/Masterfile; 33: (c) Papilio/Alamy; 34: (c) Lisa Moore/Alamy; 35: Heidi & Hans-Jurgen Koch/Minden Pictures; 36: © Masterfile (Royalty-Free Div.); 37: © John Watkins/Frank Lane Picture Agency/CORBIS; 38: © Peter Arnold, Inc./Alamy; 39: © Bach/zefa/Corbis; 40: Phil A. Dotson/Photo Researchers, Inc.; 68: image100/Alamy; 69: David Gowans/Alamy; 70-71: Joe McDonald/CORBIS; 72: Photodisc/Getty Images; 73: Peter Arnold, Inc./Alamy; 74: © Ben Van Den Brink/Foto Natura/Minden Pictures; 74-75: Wildscape/Alamy; 116: Dr. Merlin Tuttle/BCI/Photo Researchers, Inc.; (bkgd) Don Farrall/Getty Images; 117: Fred Bruemmer/Peter Arnold, Inc.; (bkgd) Don Farrall/Getty Images; 118: (bkgd) Don Farrall/Getty Images; 118-119: Virginia P. Weinland/Photo Researchers, Inc.; 119: © Dr Merlin Tuttle/BCI/Photo Researchers, Inc.; (bkgd) Don Farrall/Getty Images; 120: (bkgd) Don Farrall/Getty Images; 120-121: (t) Dinodia Images/Alamy; 121: © Bruce Coleman Brakefield/Alamy; (bkgd) Don Farrall/Getty Images; 122: Danita Delimont/Alamy; (bkgd) Don Farrall/Getty Images; 122-123: Gerard Lacz/Peter Arnold, Inc.; 123: (bkgd) Don Farrall/Getty Images; 124: (l) Joe Blossom/Photo Researchers, Inc.; (tr) Fletcher & Baylis/Photo Researchers, Inc.; (bkgd) Don Farrall/Getty Images; 128: (b) BananaStock/Alamy; 129: Nigel Cattlin/Alamy; 130: Sergio Sade/Getty Images; 131: Fernando Bueno/Getty Images; 133: Maximilian Weinzierl/Alamy; 134-135: Peter Arnold, Inc./Alamy; 135: © Robert Clay/Alamy; 136: Jeremy Woodhouse/Masterfile; 176: © imagebroker/Alamy; 177: Laureen March/CORBIS; 178: Bildagentur Franz Waldhaeusl/Alamy; 179: Ingemar Edfalk/Alamy; 180: Visual&Written SL/Alamy; 181: Dacorum Gold/Alamy; 182: Tom McHugh/Photo Researchers, Inc.; 183: Reinhard Dirscherl/Alamy; 184: (l) Ingemar Edfalk/Alamy; (r) Dacorum Gold/Alamy; 212: Julie Habel/CORBIS; 213: Scott Olson/Getty Images; 214: Dennis Macdonald/Index Stock Imagery; 215: Larry Dale Gordon/zefa/Corbis; 216: Paul Simcock/Iconica/Getty Images; 217: Eric Nguyen/Jim Reed Photography/CORBIS; 218: StockTrek/Getty Images; 219: Burton McNeely/Getty Images; 220: Chris Lisle/CORBIS; 236: © imagebroker/Alamy; 237: Jeff Rotman/Alamy; 238: Manfred Danegger/Peter Arnold, Inc.; 239: C & M Denis-Huot/Peter Arnold, Inc.; 240: Joseph Van Os/Getty Images; 241: Peter Arnold, Inc./Alamy; 242-243: Joel Sartore/National Geographic/Getty Images; 243: Stock Connection Distribution/Alamy; 244: IT Stock/PunchStock; 296-297: Tom Stewart/CORBIS; 297: (t) Emilio Ereza/Pixtal/AGEfotostock; 298: Brand X Pictures/Getty Images; 299: A&P/Alamy; 300: (bl) Alan L. Detrick/Photo Researchers, Inc.; (tr) Jerome Wexler/Photo Researchers, Inc.; 301: David Cavagnaro/Peter Arnold, Inc.; 302: Jeff Lepore/Photo Researchers, Inc.; 303: PhotoLink/Getty Images; 304: Altrendo Images/Getty Images; 332: Gabe Palmer/CORBIS; 333: POPPERFOTO/Alamy; 334: Digital Vision/SuperStock; 335: NASA/Roger Ressmeyer/CORBIS; 336: NASA/Photo Researchers, Inc.; 337: StockTrek/Getty Images; 338: © NASA/JPL/Handout/Reuters/Corbis; 339: Brand X Pictures/PunchStock; 340: Atlas Photo Bank/Photo Researchers, Inc.; 344-345: Murat Taner/zefa/Corbis; 345: Edward Hattersley/Alamy; 346: Joel W. Rogers/CORBIS; 347: Philip James Corwin/CORBIS; 348: Michel Friang/Alamy; 349: plainpicture/Alamy; 350: FORESTIER YVES/CORBIS SYGMA; 351: FORESTIER YVES/CORBIS SYGMA; 352: allOver photography/Alamy.